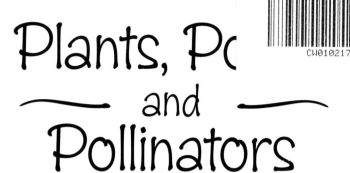

Plants, Po and Pollinators

Written by Becca Heddle

Contents

Collins

Plants and pollen

Every living thing needs to **reproduce** so it doesn't die out. To do this, flowering plants make seeds.

In order to make seeds, most flowers need **pollen** from another flower. The pollen has to get inside the **stigma** to **fertilise** the flower. Then the fertilised cells grow into seeds.

The pollen needs to get inside the stigma.

stigma

pollen grains

Pollen can't move on its own – it needs something to transfer it to the stigma of another plant. Sometimes the wind does this, but most flowering plants are helped by some kind of creature. The scientific name for these pollen porters is pollinators.

Let's find out about the range of creatures that flowers use as pollinators.

Fact

Plants are very useful to humans as they provide food and shelter. So it's important for us that pollinators do their jobs.

The main pollinators

Bees are the top pollinators in the world. They are responsible for pollinating nearly three-quarters of the plants that make food for humans, and many more that don't.

Bees feed from grapefruit flowers.

But bees don't visit flowers out of kindness – they are looking for food for themselves. Both pollen and **nectar** are important food for bees.

Nectar is sweet and sticky like sugar syrup. It is a bee's main source of energy.

This bee is drinking nectar from a cucumber flower.

4

Honeybees have pollen baskets on their back legs.

Pollen is a bee's source of protein – like meat, fish, cheese or nuts are for us.

Whenever a bee collects food from a flower, pollen sticks to its furry body. It's this pollen that pollinates other flowers. The pollen falls off into the stigma of the next flower the bee visits.

Bees mainly visit flowers with petals that are easy to land on, like this foxglove.

Pretty-winged pollinators

Bees aren't the only flying insect to pollinate plants – almost as famous are butterflies.

Like bees, butterflies are searching for nectar. But their big wings mean they can't crawl right inside the flowers. Instead, they use their long tongues to collect the nectar.

Butterflies usually feed on flowers they can stand on. Pollen from the flowers sticks to their legs and bodies, and rubs off into other flowers.

Buddleia is sometimes called "butterfly bush" because it attracts so many butterflies.

Moths are very similar to butterflies, except they are mainly **nocturnal**. So moths pollinate flowers which open when it gets dark.

Yucca moths pollinate the yucca plant of North and Central America. The moth makes a ball of pollen and pushes it into the stigma. Then it lays its eggs in the same place. The moth's **larvae** eat some of the seeds the pollen helps to make, but the plant keeps the rest.

Unpopular pollinators

Some insects that people often dislike are very useful pollinators.

bee

wasp

Just like bees, wasps feed on nectar and pollinate plants.

Fig wasps are the fig flower's only pollinator, and they work in a very unusual way. A fig's flowers are right inside the fruit.

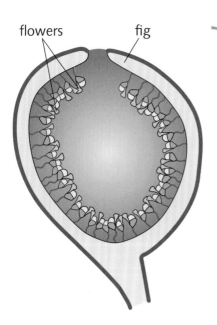

flowers   fig

Fact

Because wasps aren't as furry as bees, they can't move as much pollen around.

The tiny fig wasp crawls inside the fruit to lay its eggs. As the wasp moves around, pollen that's stuck to its body rubs off into the flowers.

8

Another unpopular insect that's a very useful pollinator is the fly.

The tropical rafflesia flower attracts carrion flies with its browny-red colour and its smell of rotting meat! The flies transfer the pollen when they lay their eggs in the flower.

Midges are tiny, biting flies. But chocolate lovers should thank them, because they pollinate cocoa plants!

The cocoa flowers hang down to let the midges in.

9

Hidden wings

There's one more winged insect that pollinates plants: beetles. A beetle's wings are hidden under hard wing-cases.

A jewel beetle with its wing-cases closed and when flying.

Fact

Beetles are the oldest known pollinators. They've been doing it for 200 million years!

Some of the oldest **species** of plants, such as magnolia, rely on beetles for pollination.

There are many different kinds of beetles, and they pollinate most of the world's flowering plants.

Beetles rely on their sense of smell to find food and places to lay eggs.

Hydnora africana

This strange-looking flower smells of dung, which is some beetles' favourite food! The beetle crawls inside the closed flower, but it's very difficult for it to get out again. Any pollen on the struggling beetle is rubbed off into the flower. The beetle is then thoroughly coated in new pollen before the flower opens a few days later.

11

Hovering pollinators

Hummingbirds' wings move so fast that they can hover. This means they don't need a place to land, so they can feed from flowers that have more unusual shaped petals. They simply hover near to the flower and push their long, curved beaks right inside to reach the nectar.

After feeding, the hummingbird's face is dusted with pollen, ready to take to the next flower.

Hummingbirds' wings move so fast, it's hard to see them.

Unlike beetles, hummingbirds don't have a very strong sense of smell. So they rely on their eyesight. The flowers they pollinate are usually brightly coloured.

Hummingbirds may be small but they need lots of food. Beating their wings 70 times a second uses a lot of energy, so they have to eat several times their own weight in nectar every day. They also eat small insects, for protein.

More bird pollinators

Hummingbirds aren't the only birds that pollinate plants. Others include parrots, sunbirds and honeyeaters.

The rainbow lorikeet feeds on nectar and pollen.

In South Africa, sunbirds pollinate milkweed flowers. These flowers look as if they are completely closed, but the sunbird's tongue can reach right inside to drink the nectar. As it feeds, the sunbird passes on pollen grains that have attached to grooves in its tongue.

This sunbird is feeding from a fuchsia flower.

Many species of honeyeaters love to be in a group.

a honeyeater's tongue

Honeyeaters are mainly found in Australia, New Zealand and the south-west Pacific. There are many different species of honeyeater but they all have one thing in common – a tongue with a tip like a brush. They use it to sweep up pollen and nectar.

Most honeyeaters live in treetops, where flowering branches provide them with food.

Honeyeaters have strong feet with sharp claws to help them grip on to plants.

Leathery wings

Bats pollinate many fruit-bearing plants, including mango, banana and peach trees. They are responsible for pollinating more than 300 plant species. Most of these plants grow in **tropical** countries in Asia, in Africa and on islands in the Pacific Ocean.

Because bats are nocturnal, they pollinate flowers that are open at night.

Bats feed on nectar from plants and pick up pollen on their faces. They also eat insects that live in the flowers.

Mexican long-tongued bat

Some bats are record-breakers!

The Mexican long-tongued bat **migrates** over 1,500 kilometres each spring. It follows the plants it feeds from, which flower as the warm weather spreads north.

This bat's record-breaking tongue is one and a half times the length of its body. In comparison to its size, it has the longest tongue of all **mammals**. When it's not feeding from flowers, it keeps its tongue rolled up inside its body.

Scaly pollinators

Lizards are important pollinators, especially on **isolated** groups of islands.

On an island off Brazil, the Noronha skink laps nectar from the mulungu tree's flowers. In the dry season, when the tree flowers, there's no natural fresh water on the island so the skink drinks nectar instead. As the skink drinks, the flower's pollen sticks to its scales. The skink takes this pollen to other flowers as it moves on to find more nectar.

Fernando de Noronha

Brazil

a Noronha skink

The blue-tailed day gecko lives on the island of Mauritius.

Indian Ocean

Mauritius

The gecko eats the nectar of the Trochetia flower. Most of the rare Trochetia plants grow surrounded by palm-like shrubs. In the open, away from the shrubs, the gecko risks being attacked by kestrels, its main **predator**. So the geckos stay amongst the shrubs and pollinate the flowers that grow there. That's why very few Trochetia grow in the open.

Little furry pollinators

Pollen sticks very well to bees' fur, making them very successful pollinators. So it shouldn't be a surprise to find out that some small mammals are pollinators, too.

a bee's fur

Nectar isn't the main food source for most mammals. But they do like sweet things!

a shrew's fur

The elephant shrew uses its long nose and tongue to get into the South African Pagoda lily for nectar. As it does this, its furry face gets covered in pollen.

an elephant shrew

20

The sugar glider has a **gliding membrane** that spreads from its wrists to its ankles.

The sugar glider is a tiny nocturnal **marsupial** that's found in Australia. It eats insects, tree sap, pollen and nectar.

When it feeds on nectar, the sugar glider's whiskers and fur pick up pollen, which it passes on to the next flower it visits.

More furry pollinators

The honey possum can be found in Australia. It's tiny, only weighing about the same as two teaspoons of sugar. It feeds on nectar and pollen alone. It's the only non-flying mammal to do this.

It has a gripping tail so it can hang from branches to seek out flowers, which it pollinates as it feeds with its long, brush-ended tongue.

Fact

Honey possums have been living in Western Australia for more than 50 million years.

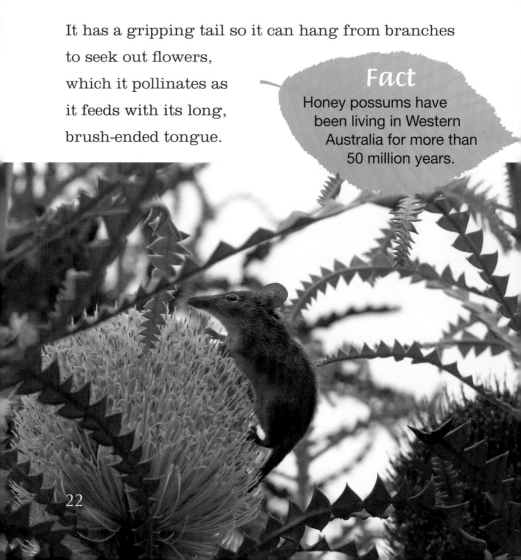

The largest pollinator of all is the black and white ruffed lemur. It uses its hand-like paws to open flowers, so it can stick its snout in to get the nectar.

Pollen sticks to the fur of the lemur's face as it drinks the nectar.

Indian Ocean

Madagascar

Attracting a pollinator

An amazing range of creatures help to pollinate flowers – but the plants also have an important job to do. Every plant has to catch the attention of a suitable pollinator. Every kind of flowering plant has features that attract its pollinator and make its job easier.

Nectar is a key attractor. Many pollinators, such as bees and hummingbirds, need nectar to survive, while others just love the taste of it!

Flowers that attract birds are often very brightly coloured to help the birds spot them. However, flowers that attract nocturnal creatures, such as bats, are often very pale, so they show up in the dark.

To guide in bees and other insects which can see **ultraviolet light**, some flowers have ultraviolet marks that humans can't see.

human view

bee's view

The ultraviolet markings show the way to the nectar and pollen.

What if it all goes wrong?

In Southwest China, people rely on the apple crop, but there are very few bees in that area today. Without bees to pollinate the apple blossom, there'd be no apples for people to eat and sell. So people go around the trees with pots of pollen and paintbrushes, dipping a pollen-filled brush into each flower.

The Brighamia insignis plant can be found in Hawaii.

All the natural pollinators of the Brighamia insignis plant have died out. To save the plant from extinction, volunteer pollinators **abseil** down cliff faces to pollinate the plants by hand.

Many pollinators are threatened by changes to the climate, loss of **habitat**, or **pesticides** used in farming which can kill them. Losing pollinators, means losing plants, including many plants that produce food for humans. People are becoming more aware of how important our natural pollinators are and the need to protect them.

Glossary

abseil move down a steep surface using a rope fixed at the top

fertilise make seeds able to grow into new plants

gliding membrane a flap of skin which stretches out when the animal leaps, so that it can glide down through the air, almost like flying

habitat the place an animal or plant lives

isolated far from other places

larvae grubs, which are baby insects

mammals animals which have live young instead of eggs, and which make milk to feed them

marsupial a mammal which has a pouch to carry its young

migrates travels to a new place to live depending on what season it is

nectar sweet liquid made by a plant

nocturnal active at night, rather than in the day

pesticides chemicals used to kill bugs on plants

pollen yellow powder made by a flowering plant

predator a creature which hunts and eats another

reproduce make new versions of itself

species a kind or type of animal or plant

stigma part of a plant that receives the pollen

tropical near the equator, where the weather is warm all year round

ultraviolet light a light that can't be seen by the human eye

Index

Finding the perfect match

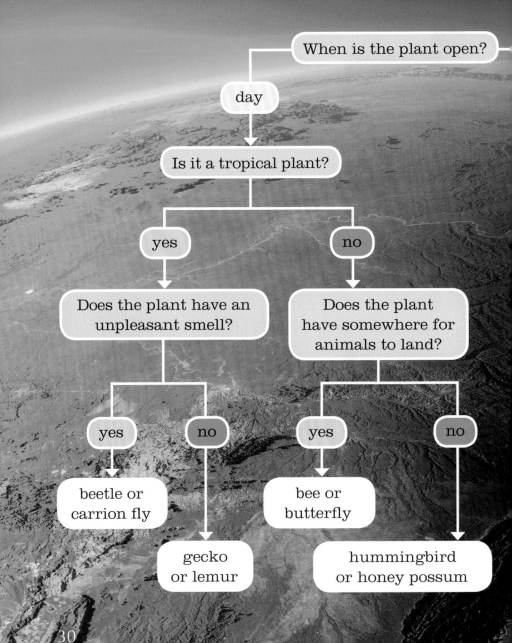

When is the plant open?

day

Is it a tropical plant?

yes

no

Does the plant have an unpleasant smell?

Does the plant have somewhere for animals to land?

yes

no

yes

no

beetle or carrion fly

gecko or lemur

bee or butterfly

hummingbird or honey possum

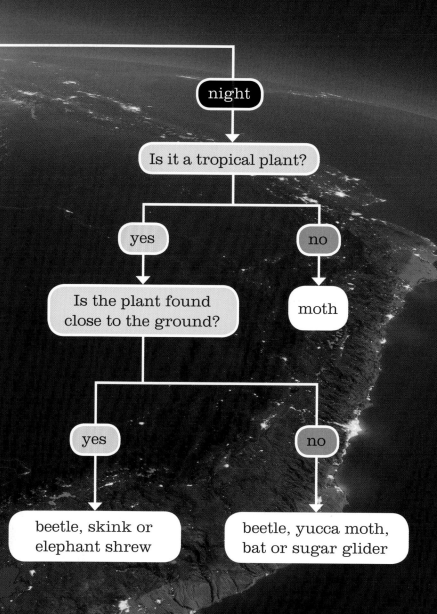

night

Is it a tropical plant?

yes

no

Is the plant found
close to the ground?

moth

yes

no

beetle, skink or
elephant shrew

beetle, yucca moth,
bat or sugar glider

Ideas for reading

Written by Clare Dowdall, PhD
Lecturer and Primary Literacy Consultant

Reading objectives:
- retrieve and record information from non-fiction
- read for a range of purposes
- identify main ideas drawn from more than one paragraph and summarise ideas

Spoken language objectives:
- give well-structured descriptions, explanations and narratives for different purposes

Curriculum links: Science – plants

Resources: outline of a bee on a whiteboard.

Build a context for reading

- Inside an outline of a bee, ask children to note any ideas that they have about pollination.
- Hand out the books and read the covers together. Decide whether children's ideas were correct or not.
- Look at the words: pollen, pollinate, and pollinators. Discuss how they are linked and notice how the spelling changes with function. Try to construct a sentence that includes all three words, e.g. a pollinator pollinates using pollen!

Understand and apply reading strategies

- Turn to the contents and read them through together. Ask children to deduce what some of the pollinators may be. What might pretty winged pollinators be?
- Ask a volunteer to read p2 aloud to the group. Ask another volunteer to recount the information using the image on p2. Support children to use technical vocabulary from reading and the image to explain how plants make seeds.